Privacy & Biometrics: Building a Conceptual Foundation

Contents .... Page

I. Introduction

The discrete fields of privacy and biometrics each have a rich history and an exciting, robust, present day status. Both disciplines are dynamic and multimodal. The current state of each is ever-changing and accelerating, and presents both promise and questions regarding its impact on individuals and societies. Much has been written on each topic, covering a breadth of issues and depth of details. Every day, new stories appear of new applications and new theories of both privacy and biometrics.

In an effort to complement and support the vibrant growth of both fields, this paper seeks to connect privacy and biometrics at a structural level so that both fields can be understood within a common framework. This paper is specifically not intended as a comprehensive collection of in-depth details about privacy or biometrics. Instead, this paper provides a general overview of both privacy and biometrics and offers a perspective through which to view the convergence of both. The goal is to provide a context in which details and future developments can be placed and better understood. The paper is organized into three primary sections.

The first section of the paper presents a high-level introduction of biometrics. The discussion explains the dual use of the term "biometrics," as referring to both physical characteristics and information processing and summarizes the general structure of biometric systems. Core terminologies and traditional as well as emerging biometric technologies are explained. This discussion concludes with a presentation of a functional architecture for understanding all biometric technologies. This functional architecture is later matched with the functional architecture of privacy to present a single framework for understanding the issues of the privacy of biometrics.

The second section of the paper presents a review of privacy, points to multiple definitions of the term "privacy" (similar to the definition of "biometrics") and highlights the conceptual foundation underlying the full scope of privacy as applied to technology. Just as with the biometric section, the privacy discussion concludes with a functional architecture that could be used as a context for understanding how to apply privacy to all information technologies.

The third section of the paper brings the two earlier discussions together applying the functional architecture of privacy to the functional architecture of biometrics. For each structural element of biometrics, the relevant portion of the privacy framework is applied and discussed. The integration of privacy and biometrics through interlaced functional architectures provides a conceptual foundation for designing and deploying privacy protective biometric systems without compromising efficient and effective operations. Privacy protective biometric technology provides an opportunity to connect information and individuals in a way that is both reliable and respectful.

Future versions of this paper will continue to target a high-level review of the integration of biometrics and privacy. The ongoing goal is to provide a timely foundation for understanding the value of privacy protective implementation and operation of biometric technologies.

An online resource is available through www.biometricscatalog.org[1] that provides in-depth background materials for each section of this and future versions of the paper.

---

[1] "The Biometrics Catalog is a US Government sponsored database of information about biometric technologies including research and evaluation reports, government documents, legislative text, news articles, conference presentations, and vendors/consultants.", www.biometricscatalog.org.

II. Biometrics

A. Biometrics Overview

The term "biometrics" is used alternatively to describe two different aspects of the technology: characteristics and processes.[2]

- Biometrics as "characteristics" refers to measurable biological (anatomical and physiological) or behavioral aspects of the person that can be used for automated recognition.

- Biometrics as "processes" refers to automated methods of recognizing an individual based on measurable biological (anatomical and physiological) and behavioral characteristics.

A typical biometric system is comprised of five integrated components:

1. A sensor that observes characteristics and converts the observations into data that can be stored in electronic form.

2. Signal processing algorithms that perform quality control activities on the collected data and develop biometric template (see below discussion entitled "Biometric Template").

3. A data storage component[3] that manages all of the data collected, including data from the initial and all future collections and processing.

4. A matching algorithm that compares the new biometric template to one or more templates that may already be stored.

---

2 NSTC Subcommittee on Biometrics, "Biometrics Overview" 7 February 2006.

3 Here, "storage" is presented as a single "component." In practice, physical storage of data may be distributed across multiple physical devices in multiple geographic locations. For purposes of discussing the elements of a whole biometric system, it is useful to discuss storage as a single element. When conducting a detailed assessment of a particular use of biometric technology, it is vital that the specific distribution, location, and control over the physical data be fully articulated.

---

5. Finally, a decision process (either automated or human-assisted) that uses the results from the matching component to make a system-level decision.

The accuracy of a biometric system is determined through a series of tests beginning with an assessment of matching algorithm accuracy (technology evaluation), and then assessing performance in a mock environment (scenario evaluation), followed by live testing on-site (operational evaluation) before full operations begin. If done properly, users will know to a high degree of accuracy how the system will perform. Even with matches that are highly probable there is still a possibility that the match is not, in fact, a match.

These tests are statistical with the results phrased in terms of probabilities rather than absolutes. As long as there is a possibility that a probable match is not an actual match, designers, managers and reviewers (privacy, security, and others) should prepare educational materials for the end users of the system and contingency plans for decisions based on matches that ultimately prove to be inaccurate.

A privacy protection analysis would focus on the level of the individual end user's understanding of the system upon first choosing to participate in the system (assuming participation is voluntary) and the actions taken regarding that individual based on matching conducted by the system. If the probability-driven nature of the system is not accommodated both in the up-front understandings between the end user and the organization administering the system and the ultimate actions taken by the organization, then the individual's decision to contribute personal information to the process and to be affected by the decisions based on that information may be compromised, calling into question the propriety of the system.

B. Terminology

Biometric terms such as "recognition," "verification" and "identification," are used interchangeably in some texts. This incorrect overlap creates confusion as each term has a unique definition. A brief description of these key terms is provided here. Additional information can be found in a glossary of biometric terms, published by the NSTC.[4]

1.   Enrollment

Biometric systems typically involve comparing a new set of biometric data with an existing set of previously-collected biometric data.[5] Enrollment is the association of previously collected biometric data with an individual.

2.   Biometric Template

A biometric template is a digital representation of one or more of an individual's distinct physical and/or behavioral characteristics. The template represents the information extracted from a biometric sample. (The biometric sample is the electronic data generated from the observation of the characteristics.)

Biometric systems generally use templates to conduct comparisons. Templates can vary between biometric modalities as well as vendors and not all biometric devices are template-based.

Some systems are labeled "biometric systems" but only store images of the characteristics — a picture of the fingerprint or of the face — instead of a template extracted from the detailed observations. These systems are generally used to assist human-driven comparisons such as those in which a screening officer may compare an image of the

---

4 NSTC Subcommittee on Biometrics, "Biometrics Glossary" 7 February 2006.

5 The National Science and Technology Council's Subcommittee on Biometrics defines "enrollment" as "The process of collecting a biometric sample from an end user, converting it into a biometric reference, and storing it in the biometric system's database for later comparison."

individual on the surface of an identification card with the individual's appearance in the image stored inside the card.

A true biometric system in the technical sense uses automated comparisons of electronic data to calculate a match. These authentic biometric systems typically use template data to conduct the match.

Template data is a smaller amount of data extracted from the detailed sample. For purposes of planning and assessment, the differential between the template and the sample is conceptually similar to the potential gap between probable match and actual identicalness. Education and contingencies should be made part of an organization's use of the system. Just as with the evaluation of the statistical nature of the overall matching, a privacy protection analysis would focus on the awareness of the participant and the sophistication of the organization's decision-making process to determine how this gap is explained and incorporated into the overall process. The technology itself may have certain limits; the integration of awareness should not.

There may be systems that are used for a more limited purpose: to offer a suggestion of possible match to a trained human examiner who then compares the raw images. In these situations, where the automated matching of template data is only used to inform a separate determination made by an expert, the privacy analysis would focus on the weight of the system's recommendation in the decision-making process of the trained expert.

3.   Recognition

Recognition is a generic term and does not necessarily imply either verification or identification (two specific terms, discussed below). All biometric systems perform "recognition" to "again know" a person who has been previously enrolled.

4. Verification

Biometric systems conduct verification by comparing a new biometric to one or more biometrics previously enrolled in the system.[6] Typically, this process involves collecting a sample, converting that sample into a template and comparing that template to other templates that were previously collected.

Verification is used to confirm whether an individual is who he or she claims to be. This type of transaction is usually connected to a process governing physical and/or logical access to an organization's resources.

There are two primary measurements of the effectiveness of verification:

■ Verification Rate: The rate at which legitimate end users are correctly verified.

■ False Acceptance Rate: The percentage of times a system produces a "false accept." A false accept occurs when an individual is incorrectly matched to another individual's existing biometric.

For planning and oversight purposes, it is important to understand the specific meaning of the phrase "whether an individual is who he or she claims to be." The individual has an identity outside the system. The system does not determine who the individual is in the global, absolute sense. The system makes a very specific, very narrow judgment as to the probability of a match between the new biometric template and an existing biometric template that was previously collected. If there is a certain level of statistical matching the system concludes that the

---

6 NSTC Subcommittee on Biometrics, "Testing and Statistics" 7 February 2006.

individual who originally enrolled is the same individual who is now facing the system.

Understanding the difference between absolute identity and system-specific identity is important when managing and evaluating a given biometric system. The enrollment process is the authoritative point of correlation for the system. There is no technical method to guarantee that the biographical information (the description of who the person is: name, address, etc.) originally associated with the biometric in fact belongs to the individual who is (in the absolute sense) that person in the absolute sense. At some point, a user (such as a system administrator) must decide what biographic information to insert into the system. This decision is not absolutely controllable through technology and thus represents a possible gap in the ultimate accuracy and reliability of the system (just as with the sample-to-template gap and the matching statistics gap).

A privacy protection analysis of the verification process would examine how rigid the organization's reliance is on the system's conclusions. If the system announces a match and proclaims a certain identity based on that match, the issue is how flexible the organization would be if the individual person disagrees with the claimed match. In determining to "absolute" identity of the individual, the issues would include:

■ Whether the claims of the system are trusted above the claims of the individual?

■ Whether the individual is given the opportunity to refute the conclusion of the system. Is it clear to both the individuals and the organization that the determination of "whether an individual is who he or she claims to be" is specifically limited to mean "do the two biometric templates match within an established parameter of statistical probability?" Put more simply: Is the data similar enough to grant the individual access?

▪ Technology is still limited and an understanding of these limits should be incorporated into the actual interactions between the individual and the organization.

5.   Identification

Biometrics systems engage in "identification" when they attempt to determine the identity of an individual end user. The identification process involves collecting a biometric, generating a biometric template and comparing the template to an entire collection of existing biometric templates.

Identification is used to determine whether or not a person is "known." This can be valuable information, particularly in situations where an organization cannot or for various reasons chooses not to ask the individual to identify him or herself. There are two primary categories of identification: Open set and closed set.

▪ Open-Set

In "open-set" identification (sometimes referred to as a "watchlist") there is no guarantee that a record of the individual's biometrics is contained in the existing set of biometric within the organization's data collection. In order to identify the new biometric, the system must search for a match across the entire data collection. There are two measurements of accuracy for open-set identification systems:

▪ False Alarm Rate: The rate at which the system incorrectly announces a match when, in fact, the individual's biometrics are not in the data collection or when the system incorrectly announces a match when the biometrics do match but the individual is not, in fact, the same individual referenced in the existing biometric record.

- Detection and Identification Rate: The rate at which the system correctly announces a match between the individual's biometrics and those biometric records previously collected.

- Closed-Set

Identification is "closed-set" if the individual's biometrics are known to exist in the database. The primary method of assessing the accuracy of a closed-set identification system is the "Identification Rate," the rate at which an individual in a database is correctly identified.

6.   Verification & Identification

Verification and identification are related processes. Verification involves the comparison of a single template to another single template (the asserted identity by the individual is used to select the existing template to compare). Identification seeks, in effect, to reverse this process by using the new template and all of the existing templates to determine the identity of the individual facing the system.

Just as with verification, in conducting identification, the system is only technically able to determine within a given statistical probability whether the new template does or does not match existing templates. Although the label "identification" is used, the specific activity that takes place is an automated comparison based on statistical probabilities. The management, oversight and assessment of the process and effect of an identification system should include awareness of the statistical nature of the matching process and should integrate that awareness into policies and procedures that frame use of the system.

C. Biometric Modalities

Different types of biometric technologies focus on different physical characteristics. Within the biometric community, these different applications are referred to as "modalities."

There is no single biometric modality that is best for all implementations. Commonly implemented or studied biometric modalities include: Fingerprint, face, iris, voice, signature and hand geometry. Many other modalities are in various stages of development and assessment.

Many factors must be taken into account when implementing a biometric system, including but not limited to: Location, security risks, task (identification or verification), expected number of end users, user circumstances, and existing data. Each biometric modality has its own strengths and weaknesses that should be evaluated in relation to the application before implementation. The effectiveness of a particular implementation of biometric technology is dependent on how and where the technology is used.

Key decision factors for selecting a particular biometric technology for a specific application includes but is not limited to:

- The environment;

- Throughput needs (the required speed of the transaction),

- Costs associated with obtaining and storing templates and conducting biometric recognition;

- Population size and demographics;

- Ergonomics;

- Interoperability with existing systems; and

■   Other user considerations - for instance, an access control system to a coal mine, where individuals might have very worn and/or dirty fingerprints, will not be a suitable environment for a fingerprint reader.

Careful evaluation of key decision factors plays a crucial role in the successful application of the selected technology. It is also important to note that different biometric modalities are in varying stages of maturity. Maturity is not solely determinative of which technology is best. Maturity can be an indicator of which technologies have more insights to offer the practice as a whole.

The following is a summary of the more widely-used biometric modalities:

1. Fingerprint Recognition

Fingerprint recognition is one of the most well-known and publicized biometrics.[7] The practice of using fingerprints as a method of recognizing individuals has been in use, manually, since the late nineteenth century. In the late 1960s, manual fingerprint recognition began transitioning into an automated process, due in large part to the emergence of computing technologies. Fingerprint recognition is popular because of the inherent ease in acquisition.

Fingerprints are formed from the skin's uneven surface of ridges and valleys. When recorded, a fingerprint appears as a series of dark lines that represents the high, peaking portion of the ridged skin; the white space is the valley (the low, shallow portion of the ridged skin) between the ridges. Ridges do not always form long and continuous patters. Often, ridges are shorter and stop and start abruptly. The result

---

7 NSTC Subcommittee on Biometrics, "Fingerprint Recognition" 7 February 2006; See also: NSTC Subcommittee on Biometrics, "Biometrics Overview" 7 February 2006.

is a unique pattern of specific characteristics such as ending ridges or dividing ridges and dots. The flow of the overall ridges is used to assign a fingerprint classification (loops, whorls, etc.). Minutiae information — the location, direction and orientation of the ridge endings and bifurcations (splits) along a ridge path — are then gathered and used to develop the fingerprint template.

One of the essential components in the field of fingerprint recognition is the development of technical standards. This focus on standards development is driven by the vast variety of algorithms and sensors available on the market. Interoperability is related to technology standards and is another crucial aspect of product implementation. Templates obtained by one system must be capable of being interpreted by a computer using another system.

To fulfill part of a USA PATRIOT ACT mandate in 2003, the US Government completed the Fingerprint Vendor Technology Evaluation (FpVTE) to evaluate the accuracy of fingerprint recognition systems.[8] FpVTE was designed to assess the capability of fingerprint systems to meet requirements for both large-scale and small-scale real world applications. The variables that had the clearest effect on system accuracy were the number of fingers used and fingerprint quality.

The determination of the number of fingers to be included in a set of fingerprints is informed by the details of the specific implementation of biometric technology. While a single fingerprint might prove sufficient for one application, two fingerprints may be required for another application.

As a general matter, ten rolled fingerprints will always present the greatest potential for the highest accuracy. It takes longer to collect

---

8 FpVTE 2003, "Fingerprint Vendor Technology Evaluation" 6 July 2004 <http://fpvte.nist.gov>.

ten rolled fingerprints and given the law enforcement community's history of collecting this type of fingerprint, there may be a certain social fear of stigma associated with "getting fingerprinted" in this way.

The determination of how much biometric data is needed to reach a certain level of statistical accuracy in matching is driven by the evaluation of the organization's resources to be accessed and/or the effect of the decision that would be made based on the match. A privacy protection analysis of the determination of how many fingers to include in a fingerprint set would focus on the specific nature of the decision to be based on the fingerprints. A privacy protective environment would advocate the collection of the least amount of personal information necessary to reliably drive the decision.

2. Face Recognition

Humans recognize familiar faces with considerable ease, not so with less familiar faces.[9] Since the 1960s, machine vision researchers have been developing automated methods for recognizing individuals via their facial characteristics. Unlike fingerprint recognition, there are no common standards of practice for face recognition. Multiple approaches using low resolution two dimensional images have existed for several years. Recent work in high resolution two and three dimensional images shows the potential to greatly improve face recognition accuracy.

The US Government performed multiple evaluations to determine the capabilities and limitations of face recognition biometric technologies and to encourage and direct future development (further information is available on the web: www.frvt.org.)

Given the state of face recognition technology, a privacy protection assessment would seek to identify the implementation

---

9 NSTC Subcommittee on Biometrics, "Face Recognition" 7 February 2006; See also: NSTC Subcommittee on Biometrics, "Biometrics Overview" 7 February 2006.

options and potential match errors and use the information about these options and potential errors to inform the decision-making process of the biometric system. Limitations in technology are not in themselves absolute barriers to privacy protective system design and operations. Limitations such as lighting conditions, the quality of photographs that might be used, and varying facial expressions, should be identified, understood, and the likely effects of those limitations should be measured and accommodated so that both the individual and the organization can accurately assess the significance of the system's functioning and place the results into the proper context.

3. Iris Recognition

The iris — the colored portion of an individual's eye — is actually a muscle within the eye that regulates the size of the pupil, controlling the amount of light that enters the eye.[10] The color of the iris is determined by the amount of melatonin pigment within the muscle. Although the coloration and structure of the iris are genetically linked, the details of the iris patterns are not.

The first step in iris recognition is to locate the iris using landmark features. These landmark features and the distinct shape of the iris itself allow for imaging, feature isolation, and image extraction. To obtain a good image of the iris, recognition systems typically illuminate the iris with near-infrared light, which can be observed by most cameras but is not detectable by, nor can it cause injury to, humans. Images of the iris are used to generate a template, a set of data that maps the patterns of the iris and the location on the iris where the patterns exist.

---

10 NSTC Subcommittee on Biometrics, "Iris Recognition" 7 February 2006; See also: NSTC Subcommittee on Biometrics, "Biometrics Overview" 7 February 2006.

Having only become automated and available within the past decade (the automated method of iris recognition has existed in patent only since 1994[11]) the iris recognition concept and industry are still relatively new. Continued research and testing remains an important component of the field of iris recognition.

A privacy protection analysis would look to the reasoning for using iris recognition in a particular application and the nature and weight of matching within the system. This understanding would establish a context within which to evaluate the impact these matches may have on the decision-making practices of the organization and, ultimately, on the experiences of the individual.

4. Hand/Finger Geometry

One of the first successful commercial biometric products was a hand geometry system, debuting in the market in the late 1970s.[12] Hand geometry systems have since become popular because of the ease of use, public acceptance, and integration capabilities.

In a typical hand geometry system, an individual enters a Personal Identification Number (PIN) code to claim an identity and then places his or her hand on the system which takes a picture of the hand. The device uses a simple process to measure and record the length, width, thickness, and surface area of an individual's hand.

One of the shortcomings of the hand geometry biometric characteristic is that it is not highly unique – thus limiting the value of a hand geometry system to verification tasks only. A privacy protection analysis should refer to the process used to select the hand geometry

---

11   John   Daugman,   "Iris   Recognition   for   Personal   Identification." <http://www.cl.cam.ac.uk/users/jgd1000/iris_recognition.html>.

12 NSTC Subcommittee on Biometrics, "Hand Geometry" 7 February 2006; See also: NSTC Subcommittee on Biometrics, "Biometrics Overview" 7 February 2006.

modality to inform the participants (the individual and the organization) of the actual capabilities and limitations of the biometric technology and the correlating level of reliance that should be placed on the resulting matches made by the system.

5. Other Biometric Identification Systems

Many other identification methods are in various stages of development and/or commercialization. Some examples are included here.

a) Speaker recognition

Speaker recognition, also known as "voice recognition," is a biometric modality that uses an individual's voice for verification and/or identification.[13] For recognition purposes, speaker recognition uses models developed from an individual's speech, a feature influenced by both the physical structure of an individual's vocal tract and the behavioral characteristics of the individual.

There are two forms of speaker recognition: text dependent and text independent.

- Text dependent systems require the individual to speak a prepared text that is programmed into the system.

- Text independent systems have no advance knowledge of the content of the individual's speech.

Text dependent systems perform more efficiently. Text independent systems are more flexible and are more effective in

---

13 NSTC Subcommittee on Biometrics, "Speaker Recognition" 7 February 2006; See also: NSTC Subcommittee on Biometrics, "Biometrics Overview" 7 February 2006.

situations where the individual may be unaware of the collection or unwilling to cooperate, or where spoofing is a concern.[14]

Since 1996, the National Institute of Standards and Technology (NIST) has conducted an ongoing series of yearly evaluations called the "NIST Speaker Recognition Evaluations," which compares research efforts and encourages collaboration across the scientific community. The purpose of the ongoing evaluation is to define the current state of the art of speaker recognition technology, to cultivate the technology's growth, and to identify the most dominant and promising algorithmic approach to problems facing speaker recognition.[15]

b) Dynamic Signature

Dynamic signature measures the speed and pressure an individual uses when signing his or her name - not what the signature itself looks like.[16] Signature recognition uses multiple characteristics in the analysis of an individual's handwriting. Common dynamic characteristics include the velocity, acceleration, timing, pressure, and direction of the signature strokes – all analyzed along the X, Y, and Z axes. These characteristics vary in use and importance from vendor to vendor and are collected using contact-sensitive technologies such as Personal Digital Assistants or digitizing tablets.[17]

The characteristics used for signature recognition are almost impossible to replicate. Unlike an image of the signature, which can be replicated by a trained human forger and/or basic imaging technologies, dynamic characteristics are complex and unique to the handwriting style

---

14 Douglas A. Reynolds, "Automated Speaker Recognition: Current Trends and Future Direction" Biometrics Colloquium 17 June 2005.

15 "NIST Speaker Recognition Evaluations" 25 April 2005. NIST Speech Group 23 June 2005.

16 NSTC Subcommittee on Biometrics, "Dynamic Signature" 7 February 2006.

17 Marc Gaudreau, "On the Distinction between Biometric and Digital Signatures" CIC Enterprise Solutions <http://www.cic.com/enterprise/whitepapers/whitepaper5.asp>.

---

of the individual. Despite this major strength, the characteristics have a large intra-class variability (an individual's own signature may vary from one collection point to another) and this often makes recognition difficult.

Dynamic signature verification holds value as a widely-usable biometric because it can easily be integrated into existing systems based on the availability and prevalence of signature digitizers and the public's acceptance of the collection process. Across this broad scope of potential applications, signature recognition technology is actually very limited – it can be used only for verification purposes due to its limited uniqueness and variations in the individual's performance. Continued research and development will help to drive to full maturity the development and application of this technology.

c) Vascular Pattern Recognition

Researchers have determined that the pattern of blood vessels is individual-specific and does not change over time. Vascular Pattern Recognition is a fairly new biometric technology.[18] Near-infrared rays of light generated from a bank of Light Emitting Diodes (LEDs) penetrate the finger or hand and are absorbed by the hemoglobin in the blood. Veins, and other areas in which the rays of light are absorbed, appear as dark areas which are then used to construct patterns. These pattern are then compressed and digitized so that it can be registered as a template. The vein pattern and the template can be compared by means of a pattern-matching technique.

---

18 NSTC Subcommittee on Biometrics, "Vascular Pattern Recognition" 7 February 2006.

6. Summary

Humans exhibit many physical and behavioral characteristics. These observable attributes are, generally speaking, readily available and easily observed. Some characteristics may appear more predominantly on one individual than they do on other individuals. Some biometric collection technologies may be more advanced or standardized than others. Some individuals may be more accommodating of one collection process than others. In the final analysis, many factors must be evaluated to select the best use of the best fitting technology to deliver the expected result: The recognition of an individual and the verification or identification of identity based on that observation and previously collected information.

The assessment of biometric systems to determine the appropriate use of collected information is intimately connected to the specific features of the chosen biometric technology. As repeated many times above, one of the primary values of a privacy protection analysis is the development of an accurate context in which both the up-front and final decisions can be assessed.

The above discussion provided an overview of the attributes of individual biometric technologies. The below discussion of privacy presents a framework for evaluating the proper application of biometric technology. Following the privacy section is a discussion of the convergence of the two frameworks, technology and privacy, to create a single holistic approach to biometric system design and operation that accommodates the benefits of the technology and the applied policies of privacy protection. The proposed framework offers a structured context and method for understanding the meaning and implications of the details regarding both the biometrics, privacy. The final goal of this is to offer assistance in the implementation of efficient, effective and privacy protective biometric systems.

The next section presents an overall framework for evaluating biometric technologies.

D. Functional Architecture

The operation of biometric systems can be organized into five discrete processes.[19] Understanding the nature of these generic processes provides a structure through which specific biometric technologies can be further understood and can provide a model for how best to view the points of intersection with privacy protection policy and practice.

1.   Collection: The first step of a biometric system involves an observation, or "collection," of the biometric data. Biometrics are typically collected using a sensor, a device that observes and records the particular physical and/or behavioral characteristic. The biometric characteristic determines the choice of biometric modality and the quality of the sensor has a significant impact on the recognition results.

2.   Conversion: The second step converts and describes the observed data previously collected into a template. The mechanics of this step vary between modalities and also between vendors.

3.   Storage: The system generally includes the capacity to store the template and/or the original collected biometric data.

---

19 NSTC Subcommittee on Biometrics, "Biometrics Frequently Asked Questions" 7 February 2006; See also: NSTC Subcommittee on Biometrics, "Biometrics Overview" 7 February 2006.

---

4. Comparison: In the third step, the newly acquired template is compared with one or more templates stored in the database. The result of this comparison is a numerical score, which is fed into a decision process (either automated or human-assisted) to determine actions such as permitting access, sounding an alarm, etc.

5. Decision: The fourth and final step involves a decision process, either automated or human-assisted, that uses the results of the matching step to make a system-level decision.

These five steps present the overall architecture of all biometric systems. Through this framework, the impact of particular operations of a specific biometric technology and system can be understood by viewing that technology/system in a larger, structured context. This comparison is particularly beneficial when conducting a privacy protection assessment.

The next section of this paper presents an overview of privacy, paralleling the above overview of biometric technology, including a discussion of the functional architecture for privacy. The final section of the paper presents a model for integrating the two architectures and argues for the value of building privacy protective biometric technologies and systems.

III. Privacy

A. Introduction

"Privacy" is an umbrella term covering very different discrete areas of study and practical situations. (An overview of the range of specific applications of the term "privacy" is provided below.) As a general matter, "privacy" is claimed as an individual interest and usually arises as an assertion against other individuals or organizations to prevent interference with the individual's autonomy.

"Privacy" means more than "private" - it is not limited to keeping a secret. Most conceptions of secrecy assert that once the secret is revealed it is available for any public use (the individual "owner" of the secret loses all claims of control over the information). However, privacy claims can cover information and activities involving others (for example, bank accounts held by banks, medications known to doctors and pharmacists, etc.).

There are privacy claims to physical locations (e.g.,: the home) and to information (e.g.,: the cost of the home). Societal emphasis on particular aspects of the overall concept of privacy change over time. Robert Ellis Smith notes one perspective shift in the United States in his book, Ben Franklin's Web Site: Privacy and Curiosity from Plymouth Rock to the Internet:

> [Privacy] is the desire by each of us for physical space where we can be free of interruption, intrusion, embarrassment, or accountability and the attempt to control the tie and manner of disclosures of personal information about ourselves. In the first half of our history, Americans seemed to pursue the first, physical privacy; in the second half – after the Civil War – Americans seemed in pursuit of the second, "information privacy."[20]

The article regularly cited as the birthplace of privacy conceptions in the United States, "The Right to Privacy" by Samuel Warren and Louis Brandeis, offers another example of the conceptual transition from physical place to information space. Warren and Brandeis point to the emerging technology of the day, "instantaneous

---

20 Robert Ellis Smith, Ben Franklin's Web Site: Privacy and Curiosity from Plymouth Rock to the Internet (Sheridan Books, Providence, RI, 2000) (Privacy Journal, 2004) 6.

photographs," as the preeminent threat to individual solitude and the sanctity of the home.[21]

The new photography was an information technology that enabled the collection of information about an individual (the photographic image) independent of his or her actual control and created the capability to use the collected information for any purpose (including "news" and/or "gossip") without further involvement or agreement from the individual.

This discussion from 1890 continues through 2006 and will likely extend into the future. Today, concerns focus on identity theft, data aggregation, warehousing and breaches, electronic surveillance, identity management and biometrics. The Warren and Brandeis concern led to some of the central questions of the privacy field, "What is the appropriate use of personal information?" "Should personal information be collected at all, in a particular application?" "What effect should privacy protection have on technology?" These core questions serve as guides for efforts like this paper that attempt to construct models that integrate privacy and technology in order to inform pragmatic decision-making.

B. Concepts of Privacy

As mentioned above, "privacy" is an umbrella term used to refer to different concerns and different situations. In general, these different uses of "privacy" share a common source: The individual. (There are some instances in which groups or organizations could be said to have "privacy" interests – typically these situations involve the control over information). Given the range of specific issues covered by the single

---

21   Harvard   Law   Review,   4   Harvard   Law   Review   193   (1890),
<http://www.louisville.edu/library/law/brandeis/privacy.html>.

"privacy" label, it is helpful to anchor a given discussion of "privacy" in a particular conceptual arena. At a high-level, "privacy" covers four broad concepts:

1. Decisional: This conception of privacy addresses issues related to an individual's authority to make decisions that affect the individual's life and body and that of the individual's family members such as end of life issues.[22]

2. Spatial: This conception of privacy addresses issues related to physical spaces like the home, the bedroom, etc. Concerns usually focus on the authority of the individual to determine who may enter or observe the objects and/or the activities that occur in the particular place.

3. Intentional: This conception of privacy addresses issues related to intimate activities or characteristics that are publicly visible. Concerns usually focus on the authority of the individual to bar further communication of the observable event or feature. Examples typically include claims against repeating conversations that occurred in public but were directed to specific individuals and publishing photographs of unintended nudity, etc.

4. Informational: This conception of privacy addresses issues related to the use of information that relates to an individual. Concerns usually focus on the extent of the individual's authority to control how that information is used (by whom and for what purpose) and the corresponding responsibility of other individuals and organizations to include the individual in decision-making processes that drive subsequent use.

---

22 Daniel J. Solove (with Marc Rotenberg & Paul M. Schwartz), <u>Information Privacy Law</u> 2nd edition (Aspen Publishing Co., 2006): 1.

A thorough privacy analysis of an actual application of biometric technology/system should begin with a determination of which concept, or combination of concepts, of privacy is applicable. Each concept focuses on a different area of social and legal, theory and practice.

The decision to label a situation with a particular privacy conceptualization will prioritize different aspects of the analysis and ultimately determine the direction of the privacy assessment. Perhaps the observable physical characteristic (the biometric) is collected by the government by force (decisional); or observed within an individual's home (spatial); or is a body part unintentionally revealed in public (intentional); or collected for one purpose and used for an unrelated purpose (informational); or a combination of all four. A thorough privacy assessment should identify each of these aspects and discuss them individually and holistically.

The overview of biometric technology presented above focused predominantly on how observations of physical characteristics are converted into electronic data (samples, templates, etc.) and used to drive decisions controlling access to an organization's resources. The concept that most closely fits the character of the biometric technology discussion is information privacy. As a result, the privacy discussion in this paper focuses on the concept of information privacy

C. Sources of Information Privacy

As mentioned above, a popular source of the foundational discussions of information privacy is the 19th century law review article written by Warren and Brandeis. That article is a popular source of the declared existence of an individual right to privacy. To understand the character and scope of a claim to individual information privacy it is important to look beyond this article to other sources.

This section presents an overview of a range of sources of the individual claim to information privacy and provides an overall feel for the variety of character across the various sources of information privacy and an indication of some of the concepts that inform a privacy analysis.

1.   The Article: "The Right to Privacy"

Warren and Brandeis wrote their famous article in response to two qualitative shifts in their society: technology and societal appetite. The technological advance took the form of a new handheld camera. Earlier cameras were large and slow and required the intentional participation of the subject. The new cameras were smaller and faster and made it easy for one individual to photograph another without permission or even awareness. At the same time, "gossip" newspapers erupted in popularity creating a vacuum for content about individual personal lives. New information technology (the camera) and new uses of personal information (the papers) combined to create a new situation for individuals (the publication of unintended, personal information). Warren and Brandeis responded by asserting an individual right to control the collection and use of information that would restore the proper location of control to the individual data subject.

Today many new technologies enable the observation and collection of information about individuals – biometric technologies are only one example. Today there are also many new appetites, new desired uses for collected information. When approaching a privacy assessment of a biometric system, these general concerns should be reviewed thoroughly. The analysis should contain a study of what is technically possible (data collected without the data subject's awareness), where the point of actual control is placed (with the data subject or data collector) and the particular combination of technical capability and intended use and control that are configured and communicated.

2.   The US Constitution

The US Constitution does not use the term "privacy" directly. Read as a whole, however, the Constitution does contain many prominent provisions that deliver privacy protections. These provisions include: The First Amendment protects against disclosure of group membership; the Third Amendment protects the home; the Fourth Amendment protects against unreasonable government searches of personal spaces, possessions and the body; and the Fifth Amendment protects against forced self-disclosure of information. In 1965, the US Supreme Court formally declared a Constitutional right to privacy drawn from the "zones" of freedom created by these individual rights.

Incorporating a constitutional analysis into a technology review may seem too theoretical or impractical to conduct. At a general level, however, each of the "zones" signifies a principle and a circumstance that could arise in the use of biometric data. For example, the Fourth Amendment's focus on unreasonable search and seizure includes a review of the individual's expectation of privacy. The Individual must have an actual expectation of privacy (subjective test) and that expectation must be reasonable in that circumstance (objective test). Even if a strict Fourth Amendment analysis is not triggered, an assessment of privacy expectations should be considered to better inform the development, operation and, ultimately, the acceptance of the biometric technology implementation.

The focus of the privacy analysis would likely be on the circumstances of the collection of the biometric and the full array of subsequent use of the biometric data within that system and within any other system that may share the same data. While a direct constitutional analysis will not likely appear in a routine privacy assessment, the issues and principles found in the Constitution are fundamental to our society and should inform the overall privacy analysis of a biometric system.

3.   Individual Privacy Claims

There is another aspect of privacy's history in the US that may serve as an additional source of privacy concerns: Privacy Torts. Generally speaking, torts are civil injuries for which individuals may be compensated.[23] In 1960, William Prosser surveyed roughly 300 legal cases and consolidated the various claims filed by individuals into four separate causes of action:[24]

1.   Intrusion upon the individual's private affairs;

2.   Public disclosure of embarrassing private facts about the individual;

3.   Publicity (wide-scale publication) that places the individual in a "false light" in the public view; and

4.   Appropriation of the individual's name or likeness.

Each of these claims has a history in the law. One can read the facts and the opinions of judges in actual cases to understand the detailed characteristics of each tort. It is possible that an individual could file a claim related to the use of biometric information under one of these causes of action at which point the details of what does or does not qualify and the measure of the injury would become the focus of the discussion. The four discrete torts can be reduced to three general concerns:

- Interfering with an individual's private affairs;
- Sharing embarrassing information about the individual; and Using
- someone's name or image for personal gain.

---

23 For additional information on torts, see generally, "tort" in Black's Law Dictionary (8th ed. 2004); See also: <www.law.cornell.edu/wex/index.php/Tort>.

24 Anita L. Allen-Castellitto and Richard C. Turkington, Privacy Law: Cases and Materials: (Thomson West, 2002): 58; see also William L. Prosser, "Privacy," 48 Calif. L. Rev. 383 (1960).

A privacy assessment of the design and operation of a biometric system should incorporate these concerns. The issue would not necessarily be whether an individual would succeed on a particular tort claim. Instead, the focus of the privacy assessment should be at a more general level: Does the use of the system intrude into the personal lives of individual end users? For example, if the biometric information in the system could potentially reveal medical information about the individual,[25] is that potentially embarrassing medical information being shared? How does the system control who can use biometric data for which purposes?

These torts are based in actual law suits each of which demonstrates a concern someone had about privacy violations. Understanding the nature and character of these claims will inform the designers, operators, and administrators of the types of system functions (all potential uses of data in the system) may raise heightened privacy concerns.

4.   US State Privacy Laws

Many US states, including Alaska, California, Florida, Illinois, Louisiana, and South Carolina, have expressly granted constitutional and statutory privacy rights. In addition to general grants of individual rights, many states grant additional, specific privacy rights that do not necessarily have Federal corollaries. For example, Louisiana and New Jersey protect the privacy of the home against peering through windows. Other states have more aggressive privacy laws such as California's "Database Security Breach Notification Act" that requires government and private sector organizations to notify individual customers of a system breach that may have led to the release of personal information.

---

25 International Biometric Industry Association (IBIA), "BITE project initiates a European debate on the ethics of biometrics," 16 May 2005 , <http://www.ibia.org/biometrics/industrynews_view.asp?id=49>.

New approaches like California's with broad reach and specific triggering events suggest a need for a different level of planning on the part of organizations regarding the collection and use of personal information, particularly in light of the number and volume of data breaches.[26]

Every biometric system exists within a legal jurisdiction and many may exist across multiple jurisdictions — federal, state, and local. There are different ways to identify relevant jurisdictions: By the location of the physical hardware, by the location of individual participants (including temporary or transitory locations), and/or by the location from which the system owner benefits. The laws of each place that is relevant to the system should be reviewed and incorporated into the strategy and design of system operation and administration.

5.   International Privacy Frameworks

In Europe in 1980, the Organization for Economic Cooperation and Development (OECD) issued guidelines for transborder sharing of privacy information as the first European model for implementing privacy protection laws across national borders. This model emphasized harmonizing national privacy laws to allow for efficient sharing across borders. The European Union (EU) adopted a similar holistic approach to privacy. These unifying perspectives stand in contrast to the segmented, sector-specific, approach adopted in the US (see below discussion of "Special Categories"). The Council of Europe Convention of 1950 formally declared privacy protection as a human right — a right was later embodied in the 1995 "Data Directive of the European Union," a model for processing personal information throughout the EU. More recently, in 2003, the Asia Pacific Economic Cooperation Forum (APEC) issued a set of guidelines on global data transfers of privacy information. The OECD,

---

26 Robert Ellis Smith, <u>Compilation of State and Federal Privacy Laws</u>, 2002 Edition: 1, 50-51.

EU, and APEC frameworks share principles for limiting the collection of personal information, ensuring accuracy and relevance, ensuring articulation and announcement of the purpose for the collection, use limitations, transparency or "openness" as to actual processing of personal information, "individual participation" — granting the individual data subject the right to know whether personal information is being collected about him or herself, the right to request a copy of the personal information, and the right to challenge the accuracy and necessity of the data - including the opportunity to have the data erased.[27]

Just as biometric systems may exist in multiple jurisdictions within a nation, an individual system may also cross international boundaries. International connections may exist through the physical equipment used by the system, the information contained in the system, the individuals using the system, and/or the individuals related to information that is used by the system. For system design and operation, territoriality may seem immaterial given the geographically independent nature of distributed architecture. For privacy protection, all laws across the entire footprint of the system should be accommodated and incorporated.

6.   Summary

Biometric technology and privacy both have long histories and are constantly evolving. Information technology is fueling today's privacy discussion just as it did in the 19th century. Privacy is driving a review of the fundamentals of technology in an effort to align capability with intention. Understanding the history of biometrics and the source of privacy frames the application of privacy principles to biometric

---

27 John W. Kropf, Director of International Privacy Programs, The Privacy Office, US Department of Homeland Security.

technology and through that application, identifies the potential privacy impact that could be generated by a particular implementation of biometric technology.

The biometric discussion presented a functional architecture into which an equivalent architecture of privacy can be integrated. The remaining steps are to build the functional architecture for privacy and then fit the two together to offer a conceptual foundation for the development and operation of biometric systems.

The following discussion presents an overview of the core of information privacy which serves as the foundation for the functional architecture of information privacy.

D. Information Privacy

Information privacy focuses on a specific type of information: "Personal Information." As a general matter, privacy is an individual interest which suggests that the information at issue should be somehow connected to the individual. The term "personal information" represents exactly that type of information.

1. Personal Information

Personal information is any information that could be used in any way to identify an individual.

This definition is scoped broadly to include all information that relates to an individual (note the word "could" and the repeating word "any" in the definition). "Personal" can be driven by both content (information that itself identifies an individual — name, etc.) and intent (uses of even non-identifying data for the purpose of identifying an individual).

Data that may not appear to be "personal information" can become "personal information" through use. If data that does not directly identify an individual is used in combination with other data that also does not directly identify an individual, and if the resulting combined data could be used to identify an individual, intentionally or otherwise, then the data becomes "personal information" and privacy issues may exist and should be addressed. The privacy impact of combining data for the purpose of identifying individuals reaches as far as the intent to identify.

Biometric information is personal information through its content (biometric information is collected from an observation of the individual) and through its use (the general purpose of a biometric system is to recognize individuals). A privacy assessment of a biometric system should start with the direct use of biometric information and expand to cover all uses of all data that become part of an identification and decision-making process related to individuals. (Note how the other data becomes personal information through the connection to the biometric information.)

As a general matter, where there is biometric information there is personal information and a privacy assessment should be conducted to analyze the impact that the use of this data may have on individual privacy interests. Even though a biometric system may contain biometric data that cannot be guaranteed to identify a specific individual, the nature of biometric data and the intent in collecting that data is still covered by the definition of "personal information" definition and should trigger a privacy assessment.

Once the information is determined to be "personal information," the information privacy analysis focuses on how that information is used - specifically, whether the information is used "appropriately."

2. Appropriate Use

Appropriate use is a use founded in law or sound, legitimate public policy, is clearly articulated, previously disclosed, and related to the purpose of original collection.

The collection and use of personal information should be based on a legal authority (through law or agreement). The details of that authority should be articulated and available to the individual data subjects before the initial collection. All subsequent use (including use by other systems/organizations) should be consistent or logically connected with the authority that framed the original transaction.

One of the underpinnings of the "appropriate use" test is the concept of delegation. An individual makes an initial determination to participate in a system or program based on that individual's understanding of what he or she is giving and what he or she is getting in return. In non-voluntary situations such as law enforcement activities this delegation exists at a societal level: The individual chooses to locate within the jurisdiction governed in part by the law enforcement activities and agrees to contribute a certain amount to those law enforcement activities in order to receive the lifestyle offered in return.

An information privacy assessment of a biometric system should define the context and authority of the original collection of biometric information, demonstrate that all system functionality (including information sharing) is grounded in a legal authority, that the details were articulated and available to the individual prior to collection, and that all uses of the personal information are within the scope of the original authority.

Uses may change over time and privacy protections can be applied to evolving situations. One of the most important privacy considerations to keep in the forefront of the ongoing management of a biometric system is the fundamental requirement of information privacy: Personal information should always be used appropriately. As circumstances change, system functionality, legal authority, and user awareness and expectations must be continually aligned. The coordination of these elements is the focus and result of a successful ongoing privacy analysis.

3. Special Categories

In the US, the determination of what use is "appropriate" is also shaped by different subject matters and settings of the personal information. These additional considerations are defined by those subject matters for which there is heightened concern for how the use of information might affect individuals. The below topics represent those areas of heightened concern to privacy protection. Even if it is clear that a particular law from one of these areas will not apply to a biometric system, a thorough privacy assessment should include a review of the applicability of each topic to address any concerns, however general they may be.

- **Medical:** The medical setting and health-related information is tied directly to one of the core interests of the individual: Decisions related to individual's body. As a general matter, medical providers and related organizations must receive the consent of the individual before sharing personal information.

- **Financial:** Information related to how an individual manages his or her finances is also considered one of the most intimate areas of an individual's personal life. As a general matter, financial institutions must notify the individual before sharing personal financial information.

- **Children:** Decisions related to what information can be collected from and used about an individual's child is another of the areas of heightened privacy concerns. As an example, one of the major US child-related laws requires parental consent before operators of a website can collect personal information about a child. These same concerns may apply to a larger category of individuals who are not capable — physically or legally — to manage their own affairs.

- **Government-Held:** The collection and use of personal information by the government is another primary concern in privacy protection. There are three primary laws that apply to government-held personal information: The Freedom of Information Act that usually provides access to any government record to anyone for any purpose - subject to certain exceptions that include the protection of personal privacy; The Privacy Act of 1974 that embodies a set of fair information principles to govern the government's collection, use, and maintenance of personally identifiable information contained in a system of records; and The E-Government Act of 2002 that requires government agencies to conduct assessments of their use of information technology and the potential impact that use may have on privacy.

While biometric information does not inherently trigger any of the specific laws within these areas of heightened privacy concern, the privacy assessment of the use of biometric information within the biometric system should include at least a cursory review of the relevance of these specific topics if only to identify any potential issues that might exist. It is important to recognize that individual concerns regarding privacy protection become heightened when information used by the system relates to health and/or financial status, children or when any type of personal information is used by the government, and then to accommodate those concerns during the planning and operation of the system.

4. Summary

Privacy as a term can signify many different concepts, some overlapping at times. The extraordinary advances and popularity of information technology bring one conceptualization of privacy — information privacy — to the forefront of the privacy protection discussion. The touch point of privacy and biometric technologies is in the nature and use of information. Biometric systems use information generated from observing individuals to recognize a particular individual. Since personal information is any information that *could* be used in *any way* to identify an individual, biometric information is personal information even in those situations where the identity of the individual associated with the biometric information is unknown.

The purpose of a privacy assessment is to ensure that personal information (biometric information) is used appropriately. The determination of whether a biometric system uses personal biometric information appropriately is driven by the purpose of the system and the context in which that system operates. A thorough planning effort for the use of biometric technology should include a comprehensive privacy assessment to detail any issues that might arise during actual use. The privacy assessment should be conducted at the earliest stage of system development and throughout the life of the system and data to accommodate changes over time.

The nature of an information privacy protection assessment can best be understood through a presentation of its functional architecture. The discussion that follows presents the discrete elements of the functional architecture of information privacy and sets the stage for the structured integration of privacy protection into the implementation of biometric technology presented at the conclusion of the paper.

E. Functional Architecture

There are seven elements to a thorough privacy assessment of an information technology system. These seven elements frame the questions one would ask to determine whether a biometric system protects information privacy.

1. Current Status

All systems exist along a "life cycle." As a general matter, systems are conceived, designed, developed, tested, implemented, operated, and migrated (either redesigned to fit changing needs or dismantled). Biometric systems follow this same general path. The later in the life cycle the assessment starts, the greater the potential cost of accommodating privacy protections. If the privacy assessment of a biometric system is initiated in the earliest stages, then privacy protections can be integrated into the design of the system and evolve as the biometric system itself evolves.

2. Data (Personal Information)

As discussed above, the scope of information privacy is defined by the use of personal information. If a system does not use any information that could be used in any way to identify an individual, then it is less likely that the use of system may impact privacy protections. If non-personal data is used with the intent to identify an individual, then that data becomes personal information and the potential privacy impact of using that data should be assessed.

3. Purpose & Success

Just as the use of personal information defines the scope of a privacy assessment, the purpose and success metrics guiding the management of the system play a major role in determining the system's potential impact on privacy. A privacy assessment should examine the stated purpose of the system and compare the purpose to the underlying authority of the organization and the specific authority for the program office that manages the system. The purpose for the system should align with the program office's specific authority, and the organization's general authority.

If a system is designed for a particular purpose and a privacy assessment reveals that the system fails to advance that purpose, and/or is furthering a different purpose instead, then the collection and use of personal information may fall outside the organization's authority, and may in fact negatively impact privacy protections.

4. Function (Use)

In a privacy assessment, "use" is a companion to "data" and is measured by intended value and purpose of the result. Information privacy protection enforces the appropriate use of personal information. In order to determine whether the actual use of personal information is appropriate, a privacy review would compare the results of the use of personal information to the stated purpose and determine whether the actual use successfully achieves the stated purpose of the collection. In those situations where the privacy assessment is conducted later in the system life cycle - once the system is operational - the assessment of use would compare the actual use at the time of the assessment to the expected use as determined at the time of data collection and identify any disparity. A differential between actual and anticipated use that is not supported by a demonstrated support path showing a correlating shift in expectations (and possibly authority) may indicate that the system is negatively affecting privacy protection. The gap will certainly indicate that privacy reviews should be more closely integrated into the management of the system to avoid future gaps in awareness.

5. Technology

Biometric technology raises privacy concerns primarily because of the personal nature of biometric information. Other technologies also raise privacy concerns either through the nature of the information collected or through the use of personal information. Examples of these other "privacy sensitive technologies" include radio frequency identification technology (the potential for inventorying and tracking individuals without notification) and datamining (the potential for using personal information from divergent sources for unarticulated purposes). A privacy assessment of a biometric system should identify any uses of these other technologies and accommodate any additional issues that arise.

6. Audit, Control & Access

A privacy review should include an assessment of the internal and administrative procedures that govern the audit of the biometric system and the level of control and access given to the individual regarding how the personal information is used. Together, these three considerations demonstrate how the system is governed and, ultimately, if personal information is used appropriately (the primary test of information privacy protection).

The audit process provides a history of system function and is another tool to evaluate actual use versus expected use. Routine reviews of audit logs should reveal any unauthorized and/or unintended uses and provide evidence that personal information was used appropriately.

The term "control" is used to refer to the authority that the individual retains regarding how personal information is used. If the system incorporates individual agreement to particular uses of personal information and the operators of the system decide to use the information for a different purpose, the privacy assessment would focus on whether the individual's agreement is again sought.

An assessment of access draws upon aspects of both audit and control and seeks to determine whether the individual is granted authority to view the personal information collected and the manner in which it is used to decide whether the actual use aligns with the individual's expectations at the point of original data collection.

7. Documentation

A privacy assessment should review all existing system documentation. A review of documentation serves two purposes. First, it identifies the understanding of what information the system collects and uses; and second, through distribution, it demonstrates the expectations that were set with those who may have privacy interests in the system. As with the other elements, a privacy assessment should compare the actual information and actual use with that in the documentation. Any gaps that are identified may indicate a potential negative impact on privacy protections.

IV. Application of Privacy to Biometric Technology

The above discussion presented an overview of biometric technology and privacy. The functional architecture sections offered frameworks for how to understand and assess the nature of a biometric system and the concerns of a privacy assessment. This portion of the discussion integrates the elements of a privacy assessment into the structure of a biometric system to offer a framework for analyzing specific biometric systems and their potential impact on privacy protection.

This section is organized according to the biometric system architecture and within each of the major components of that architecture, the relevant privacy protection elements are listed with a description of the concerns related to that aspect of the biometric system.

The privacy discussion of the "collection" portion of the biometric architecture provides more details regarding elements of the privacy analysis because collection is the initial point of contact between the individual and the biometric system. It is at this first point of contact that the entire context of the information to be collected and used should be communicated. The point of collection is also a fixed point in time when expectations can be measured. The privacy discussions in the sections following the "collection" section are shorter and primarily address additional specific areas of concern.

The elements of the privacy assessment dealing with documentation and audit, control and access are generally the same across each functional area of the biometric system. These issues are addressed in the first functional area, "collection," and are implied in the other functional areas. As a general matter, expectations are set in documentation and verified in the audit.

This framework offers a starting point for all privacy reviews of biometric systems. An actual privacy assessment of a particular biometric system may include other considerations and may emphasize different aspects of the system for heightened review.

Although it is not specifically detailed below, a privacy protection analysis should start with a determination of status of the system – the initial element of the privacy functional architecture. The earlier in the system development life cycle the privacy assessment occurs, the easier privacy protections can be integrated.

Once the system status is determined, the privacy assessment should analyze each of element of the biometric system's functional architecture. The first portion of the functional architecture of a biometric system involves the collection of biometric information.

A. Collection

The first stage of the biometric system is the collection of biometric information, which occurs in the initial enrollment and also at each instance of collection for comparison to the enrollment data.

During the initial enrollment, the privacy protection assessment should focus on the expectations of the individual choosing to enroll. The initial expectations will frame the assessment of the entire operation of the biometric system. During subsequent points of contact with the system, reasonable methods of communication should be established to both remind individuals of the purpose of the collection and to provide updates about any system changes that may impact privacy protections. It is important to conduct this assessment even for involuntary systems where there are limited or no communications regarding setting initial expectations.

As a general matter, the first place to look for communication that establishes expectation is in the system documentation.

1. Documentation

The documentation of a biometric system should describe the purpose and scope of the system, the data collected, and how that data is used. The documentation should also include all training and educational materials for operators of the system and any public material communicated to the individuals enrolling.

One of the primary principles of privacy protection is that personal information collected for one purpose should only be used for that purpose and not for other purposes. Documentation demonstrates the initial expectation of the owners, the operators, and the individual users of the system and creates a set point for the expectations that will guide future evaluations of the system. In order to manage expectations as the system evolves, the documentation should be updated and again communicated to those already "in" the system.

2. Purpose & Success

The privacy assessment of the collection of biometric information should identify, both in the documentation and in the understanding of the owners and operators of the biometric system, the purpose that the biometric system is designed to achieve and the means employed to measure the system's success in achieving that purpose.

The privacy analysis of statements of purpose should identity the organization's specific authority for pursuing the goal that the purpose advances and the scope of that authority. All data collected and used should be circumscribed by that authority as evidenced in the statement of purpose. All measures of success should be reliable and actually used in practice to verify the performance of the biometric system.

3. Data (Personal Information)

The most important issue to address during a privacy assessment of a biometric system is the nature and scope of the personal information collected. Data is presented as the third area of concern because the responses to the privacy review of the data collected by the system can be compared to cross-check responses related to both documentation and purpose.

Personal information should only be collected if it specifically advances a legitimate purpose. A privacy review of the biometric system's collection activities should reveal a determination of the minimal amount of personal information necessary to achieve the purpose, documented and communicated (as appropriate) to those using the system. If more information is collected than is necessary, there is a potential negative impact on privacy protection and the privacy review should provide both a description of the problem and a recommendation for a solution to make the biometric system privacy protective.

4. Technology

The privacy assessment should review any use of other privacy sensitive technologies. For example, the wireless transfer of biometric data. Each specific technology and combination of technologies may raise a unique set of privacy issues to address. It is crucial to identify all uses of all technologies in order to understand how personal data will be used and how any privacy risks to this data are communicated to those using the system.

5. Audit, Control & Access

Assertions of purpose, appropriate use, data limitation, and communication are important and they frame the privacy review. However, these assertions should be verified in order for the privacy assessment to be more than a transcript of the assertions themselves. One robust resource for claim verification is an audit of the actual system use.

Auditable systems log all system activity including the user, the data, and uses by the user of the data. A privacy review should examine these logs and determine whether the planned use of personal information within the biometric system matches the actual use.

If the audit log data contains information that could be used to identify an individual (which it likely will, given its purpose), this log data is also personal information and should be supported by a framework that identifies and enforces the appropriate use of that personal audit log data.

Issues related to the authority of individuals to control the use of personal information and their abilities to access that information should be examined as part of the collection stage of a biometric system. The system collects data offered by the individual and expectations set at the time of this transaction (during enrollment and subsequent collections for verification and identification) should guide the procedures surrounding the actual system. The privacy assessment should verify whether individuals are told they have a right of access to current uses and a right to control future use and then verify this through the audit logs, if possible.

B. Conversion

Conversion is the creation of a template from the observed data. The privacy assessment should review the nature of the information contained in the original observation and in the template. The privacy analysis should examine how closely the original observation can be related to the individual and how this compares to the correlation between the template data and the individual. All assertions of recognition and matching should be compared to the actual data used and the nature of the relationship with the actual individual.

C. Storage

The decision to store more personal information (the "raw" observation) or less personal information (the template data) will be driven by a determination of whether the potential for a match between the data and the individual is increased with more data. This determination would be compared to the applicability of the privacy principle of data limitation which would advocate storing the least amount of personal information that is necessary for system functionality and thus enabling the individual to vet the accuracy of the statistical match by supplying a new raw sample from which a new template could be generated and used. The capability of the technology, the shared expectations of system purpose and function, and the procedures guiding the use and significance of the system will also inform this decision and should all be made part of the privacy assessment.

The assessment of the "appropriate use" of stored personal information generally translates to an information security analysis of whether unauthorized persons access the data and the reliability of control and maintenance over the data itself.

D. Comparison

The privacy assessment of the process of comparing biometric templates focuses primarily on the understanding communicated regarding the significance of a match. In terms of the privacy architecture, this is mostly an issue of documentation and audit.

An area of privacy protection not discussed in the functional architecture section and of particular significance here, and in the "decision" section below, is the redress procedure. The system documentation should include a formalized process allowing individuals to challenge the system's match or failure to match. This process should accommodate for the statistical nature of the match and provide a mechanism to verify the match including, perhaps, the collection of additional information from the individual. This additional personal information should be used within the context that framed the initial collection, following the same model that guides the overall operation of the biometric system.

E. Decision

Biometric systems support decision-making, either to determine whether or not to grant access to a resource, or to determine how to approach an otherwise unknown person. Generally speaking, the biometric system facilitates only one aspect of the decision-making process: The recognition of the individual. Based on this recognition, the operator of the system makes a decision regarding how the individual is treated.

A privacy assessment of a biometric system should identify the details of this ultimate decision, the effect the decision could have on the individual, the opportunities to dispute this decision, and the relationship between the decision itself and the purpose of the system.

Just as the decision is the final result of the system operation, the privacy assessment of the decision is the ultimate result of the assessment of all the elements of the underlying biometric system. The conclusion of the privacy assessment of this stage should be supported by the conclusions of each supporting component assessment.

V.   The Value of Privacy Protective Biometric Systems

A. Public Concerns

Given the highly personal nature of biometric information, the very use of biometric technology may raise concerns for an individual and in general may create an environment ripe for rumor and misconception.[28]

The following is a sample of some of the more popular misunderstandings regarding the technology. In reviewing this list, it is important to note that the concerns are real and should be addressed specifically in any description of a particular biometric technology system, if only because members of the public may bring these concerns to the privacy discussion.

---

28 Paul Rosenzweig, Alane Kochems, and Ari Schwartz article entitled, "Biometric Technologies: Security, Legal, and Policy Implications," <http://www.cdt.org/security/20040621biometric.pdf>; See also: NSTC Subcommittee on Biometrics, "Biometrics Overview" 7 February 2006.

1. Biometric systems gather too much personal information.

The concern is that biometric systems collect a lot of unique personal information and use the personal information to make small decisions (a full fingerprint used to open a door). This concern goes to the feeling of a balance in exchange: Does the individual feel he or she is giving and receiving items of equal value? A thorough privacy assessment should provide a response to this concern by demonstrating a close connection between the data collected and the use of that data in the biometric system.

2. Biometrics will be collected and shared without permission or adequate explanation.

The concern is that the individual has no control over the decision to use personal information and, ultimately, to participate in decisions based upon that personal information. A thorough privacy assessment should provide a response to this concern by demonstrating the context and limits of the use of the particular personal biometric information and the role, if any, of the individual in controlling other uses of the information.

3. Biometrics can be used to track individuals.

The concern is that biometric systems are capable of watching individuals, recognizing each person based on publicly observable physical characteristics, and combining that data with information about the time and place of the observation. A thorough privacy assessment should provide a response to this concern by demonstrating the purpose of the particular biometric system – with an explanation of the system's limits, and explaining the nature and use of the system to those individuals affected, prior to the initial collection.

4. Biometrics reveals personal medical status.

The concern is that a biometric system would be used to collect personal biometric data for one purpose (recognition) and then be extended to gather more intimate personal information (extracting medical information from the biometric) without the individual's permission. A thorough privacy assessment should provide a response to this concern by demonstrating the biometric system's restricted use of collected biometric information and the verification of that limit through system audits.

    5.   Biometrics can be cut off and used.

The concern is that the individual might lose control over his or her involvement in the system if someone was able to either remove or copy the individual's body part containing the biometric. A thorough privacy assessment should provide a response to this concern by demonstrating quality controls that would protect the individual and the system from this type of attack (e.g., "liveness" detection).

    6.   Biometric technology can injure the individual.

The concern is that the physical biometric collection process could harm the individual. A thorough privacy assessment should provide a response to this concern by providing a detailed explanation of the actual collection mechanism (e.g., iris recognition uses a camera to photograph the eye, not a laser).

B. Privacy Protective Biometric System Design

The issues listed above are indications of the popular concerns regarding biometric technology. As the field of biometrics continues to develop, awareness of the technology's capabilities and limitations along with appropriate guidelines will also develop to increase understanding of the technology and direct its appropriate use.

Biometric technology is still evolving. There are significant advantages to establishing a close relationship between the individual person and data in a system. Biometric systems can improve the process of recognizing individuals and facilitate decision-making processes that require that type of recognition.

The information contained in biometric systems is, by its very nature personal - it is intimately connected to the individual. This close bond of information-to-individual triggers the need for an information privacy protection analysis to ensure that the information is used appropriately. Through the unique lens of privacy protection the larger implications of a particular system's operation can be viewed, specifically in terms of potential unintended consequences for individuals.

The overview presented in this paper summarizes the nature of biometric technologies and privacy and how to integrate the two to guide the design, creation, implementation and operation of biometric systems to deliver operational functionality in a way that respects the individual participants.

The fields of biometric technology and privacy are continually progressing. New advances in technology raise new privacy protection concerns and new decisions regarding privacy shape the policies and procedures governing biometric systems. Dialogs like the one in this paper, even at this summary level, ensure that the evolution of biometric technology and privacy advance in harmony rather than in isolation.

VI. About the National Science and Technology Council

The National Science and Technology Council (NSTC) was established by Executive Order on November 23, 1993. This Cabinet-level Council is the principal means within the executive branch to coordinate science and technology policy across the diverse entities that make up the Federal research and development enterprise. Chaired by the President, the membership of the NSTC is made up of the Vice

President, the Director of the Office of Science and Technology Policy, Cabinet Secretaries and Agency Heads with significant science and technology responsibilities, and other White House officials.

A primary objective of the NSTC is the establishment of clear national goals for Federal science and technology investments in a broad array of areas spanning virtually all the mission areas of the executive branch. The Council prepares research and development strategies that are coordinated across Federal agencies to form investment packages aimed at accomplishing multiple national goals. The work of the NSTC is organized under four primary committees; Science, Technology, Environment and Natural Resources and Homeland and National Security. Each of these committees oversees a number of sub-committees and interagency working groups focused on different aspects of science and technology and working to coordinate the various agencies across the federal government. Additional information is available at www.ostp.gov/nstc.

VII. About the Subcommittee on Biometrics

The NSTC Subcommittee on Biometrics serves as part of the internal deliberative process of the NSTC. Reporting to and directed by the Committee on Homeland & National Security and the Committee on Technology, the Subcommittee:

- Develops and implements multi-agency investment strategies that advance biometric sciences to meet public and private needs;

- Coordinates biometrics-related activities that are of interagency importance;

- Facilitates the inclusions of privacy-protecting principles in biometric system design;

▪ Ensures a consistent message about biometrics and government initiatives when agencies interact with Congress, the press and the public;

▪ Strengthen international and public sector partnerships to foster the advancement of biometric technologies.

Additional information on the Subcommittee is available at www.biometrics.gov.

A. Subcommittee on Biometrics

▪ Co-chair: Duane Blackburn (OSTP)
▪ Co-chair: Chris Miles (DOJ)
▪ Co-chair: Brad Wing (DHS)
▪ Executive Secretary: Kim Shepard (FBI Contractor)

B. Department Leads

▪ Mr. Jon Atkins (DOS)
▪ Dr. Sankar Basu (NSF)
▪ Mr. Duane Blackburn (EOP)
▪ Ms. Zaida Candelario (Treasury)
▪ Dr. Joseph Guzman (DoD)
▪ Dr. Martin Herman (DOC)

▪ Ms. Usha Karne (SSA)
▪ Dr. Michael King (IC)
▪ Mr. Chris Miles (DOJ)
▪ Mr. David Temoshok (GSA)
▪ Mr. Brad Wing (DHS)
▪ Mr. Jim Zok (DOT)

C. Social/Legal/Privacy ICP Team

Champion: Peter E. Sand (DHS Privacy Office)

Members & Support Staff:

- Mr. Duane Blackburn (OSTP)
- Ms. Zaida Candelario (IRS)
- Mr. Trent Depersia (DHS S&T)
- Ms. Mary Beth Dormuth (FAA)
- Mr. Jeffrey Dunn (NSA)
- Mr. Ed Harras (FAA)
- Mr. Phillip Loranger (DOT)
- Mr. Steve McKay (ITIC Contractor)
- Mr. Chris Miles (NIJ)
- Mr. Kenneth Mortensen (DHS Privacy Office)
- Mr. Greg Motta (FBI)
- Ms. Joyce Nyman (Coast Guard)
- Dr. Jonathon Phillips (NIST)
- Ms. Jennie Plante (DOJ)
- Mr. Robert I. Ross (DOT)
- Mr. Brandon Schneider (DoD Contractor)
- Ms. Susan Sexton (FAA)
- Ms. Kimberly Weissman (DHS US-VISIT)
- Mr. Brad Wing (DHS US-VISIT)
- Mr. Steve Yonkers (DHS)
- Mr. Jim Zok (DOT)

VIII. Special Acknowledgements

The Communications ICP Team wishes to thank the following contributors for their assistance in developing this document:

- Peter E. Sand, DHS Privacy Office, for performing exhaustive research and serving as lead author in the development of this document.

- Members of the ICP's drafting team (Duane Blackburn, Kenneth Mortensen, Robert I. Ross , Brandon Schneider, Steve Yonkers and Jim Zok) for assistance in writing the document, reviewing numerous drafts and participating in even more discussions.

- Toby Milgrom Levin and Anna Slomovic of the DHS Privacy Office for reviewing the document and providing numerous helpful comments.

IX.   Document Source

This document, and others developed by the NSTC Subcommittee on Biometrics, can be found at www.biometrics.gov.